EYE TO EYE
with Cats

Exotic Cats

Lynn M. Stone

ROURKE PUBLISHING
Vero Beach, Florida 32964

www.rourkepublishing.com

PHOTO CREDITS: © Karine Belisle, Perlexotic Cattery: 8, 13, 14; © Pam DeGolyer, Ivy Cat Cattery: 10, 12, 15, 16; all other photos © Lynn M. Stone

Editor: Jeanne Sturm

Cover and page design by Heather Botto

Library of Congress Cataloging-in-Publication Data

Stone, Lynn M.
  Exotic cats / Lynn M. Stone.
     p. cm. -- (Eye to eye with cats)
  Includes index.
  ISBN 978-1-60694-336-6 (hard cover)
  ISBN 978-1-60694-862-0 (soft cover)
  1. Exotic shorthair cat--Juvenile literature. I. Title.
  SF449.E93.S76 2010
  636.8'2--dc22

                          2009005983

Printed in the USA

CG/CG

ROURKE PUBLISHING

www.rourkepublishing.com - rourke@rourkepublishing.com
Post Office Box 643328 Vero Beach, Florida 32964

Table of Contents

Exotic Cats

The Exotic is a handsome, shorthaired cat with the body type and flattened face of longhaired **Persian** cats. The Exotic shares its warm, laid-back **personality** with Persians, too.

Exotics have broad, round faces and thick, **plush** coats. An Exotic could be mistaken for a stuffed toy animal, like a teddy bear!

An Exotic's thick coat softens its look and highlights the round appearance of its face.

The Exotic's Looks

With good reason, Exotics are often described as shorthaired Persians. The Persian **breed**, or kind, of cat is a direct **ancestor** of the Exotic.

Like a Persian, the Exotic has a **chunky**, medium to large body on short legs. It has full, furry cheeks and a moon-shaped head with small, round ears.

Judges look for small, round-tipped ears and a straight tail when assessing Exotics. A kinked tail will disqualify a cat from competition.

The Exotic has large paws and shoulders. Most Exotics have big, round eyes like golden marbles, although some Exotic's eyes are blue.

Seal point is one of many Exotic coat colors. Exotics may also be blue-cream, blue, silver, or one of several **tabby** colors.

The red tabby Exotic is growing in popularity.

A purebred Exotic cat shows the flat face of a Persian and the plush, short fur of an American shorthair.

Purebred Exotics

A cat whose parents are both of the same breed is a **purebred**. The Exotic is one of about 40 cat breeds recognized by the Cat Fanciers Association.

Purebred cats show the same features over and over again. A person who buys a purebred kitten can be fairly sure it will grow up to be much like its parents.

Those looking to buy a purebred kitten might want to visit a cattery, where experts board and breed cats.

Purebred Exotics usually are shorthaired and have quiet voices and easygoing personalities. But some are longhaired like their Persian ancestors.

Breeders use different tests to figure out which kittens are longhaired and which are shorthaired. Once they make a prediction, breeders have to wait 8-9 weeks to find out if they were correct.

A longhaired kitten from Exotic parents can be shown as a Persian or as an Exotic Longhair.

Purebred cats, like the Exotic, make up less than 10 percent of the cat population in North America. In most countries, fewer than two of every 100 cats are purebreds.

Cat organizations, among them the Cat Fanciers Association, keep track of purebred cat numbers in several places, including the United States, Canada, Japan, and several countries in Europe and South America.

Cats' exceptionally large eyes help them see well in low light.

The Cat for You?

The Exotic is a gentle, cuddly cat. It is slightly more lively and curious than its Persian cousin. It tends to choose a favorite human friend, but most Exotics are soon comfortable even with strangers.

Exotics need some **grooming**, but Persians need almost daily brushing. For this reason, the Exotic is sometimes called "a lazy person's Persian."

The first Exotics were silver, but in recent years other colors have become popular, including black, tortoiseshell, red tabby, brown tabby, and bi-color.

A red tabby Exotic gets its name from its color and its tabby stripes.

Exotics are a good fit for households where someone is usually at home. Exotics love human attention and laps. They do not like to be left alone. They are quietly playful cats and easy to groom.

Be aware that the Exotic's flat face can cause breathing and eye problems for the cat, just as it can in Persians.

Statistics from the Cat Fanciers Association confirm the popularity of the brown tabby shorthair.

Runny eyes are common to the breed, so owners of Exotics give their cats' eyes a daily wiping.

The History of Exotics

A few American shorthair **fanciers** in the 1950s wanted to improve the body shape of their cats. They also wanted to introduce the silver (white) Persian color into their breed.

The American shorthair fanciers **crossed** some of their cats with Persians. Eventually, American shorthair breeders mixed in other shorthaired breeds: Burmese, Russian Blue, and Abyssinian among them.

In 1967 the Cat Fanciers Association recognized the Persian shorthairs as a new breed, the Exotic Shorthair.

In competition, judges look for heavily boned, well balanced cats.

The name Exotic came from the addition of the new silver coat. The white coat was so different, shorthair breeders thought it exotic.

When the breed was first developed, some considered calling it Sterling, because of its beautiful silver color.

ABOUT CAT BREEDS

The beginnings of domestic, or tame, cats date back at least 8,000 years, when people began to raise the kittens of small wild cats. By 4,000 years ago, the Egyptians had totally tame, household cats. Most actual breeds of cats, however, are fewer than 150 years old. People created breeds by selecting parent cats that had certain qualities people liked and wanted to repeat. Two longhaired parents, for example, were likely to produce longhaired kittens. By carefully choosing cat parents, cat fanciers have managed to create cats with predictable qualities—breeds.

Exotic Cat Facts

- Date of Origin – 1950s-1960s

- Place of Origin – United States

- Overall Size – medium to large

- Weight – 7-14 pounds (3-6.5 kilograms)

- Grooming – twice weekly

- Activity Level – low

- **Temperament** – affectionate, curious; needs attention

- Voice – quiet

Glossary

ancestor (AN-sess-tur): those past members of a family, usually before one's grandparents

breed (BREED): a particular kind of domestic animal, such as an Exotic cat

chunky (CHUHNG-kee): short and solid

crossed (KRAWSST): to have used cats of two different breeds as parents

fanciers (FAN-see-erz): those who raise and work to improve purebred cats

grooming (GROOM-ing): the act of brushing, combing, and cleaning

Persian (PUR-zhun): a breed of cat known for its long fur and flattened face

personality (pur-suh-NAL-uh-tee): the qualities and behavior that make one person or animal different from others

plush (PLUSH): fur that is short, soft, and thick

purebred (PYOOR-bred): an animal with ancestors of the same breed

seal point (SEAL POINT): the dark brown (seal) color on the ears, tail, feet, and faces of certain cats

tabby (TAB-ee): a striped cat or the striped coat of a cat

temperament (TEM-pur-uh-muhnt): an animal's nature or personality

Index

Websites to Visit

kids.cfa.org
www.ticaeo.com
www.cfainc.org/breeds/profiles/exotic.html

About the Author

A former teacher and sports writer, Lynn Stone is a widely published children's book author and nature photographer. He has photographed animals on all seven continents. The National Science Teachers Association chose one of his books, *Box Turtles*, as an Outstanding Science Trade Book for 2008. Stone, who grew up in Connecticut, lives in northern Illinois with his wife, golden retriever, two cats, and abundant fishing tackle.